Shark vs. Killer Whale

This book is dedicated to the memory of Lucy Owen,
who really cared about this series.

ISABEL THOMAS

www.raintreepublishers.co.uk
Visit our website to find out more information about **Raintree** books.

To order:
☎ Phone 44 (0) 1865 888112
▤ Send a fax to 44 (0) 1865 314091
💻 Visit the Raintree bookshop at **www.raintreepublishers.co.uk** to browse our catalogue and order online.

First published in Great Britain by Raintree, Halley Court, Jordan Hill, Oxford OX2 8EJ, part of Harcourt Education. Raintree is a registered trademark of Harcourt Education Ltd.

Editorial: Dan Nunn and Katie Shepherd
Design: Victoria Bevan
and Bridge Creative Services Ltd
Picture Research: Hannah Taylor
and Rebecca Sodergren
Production: Duncan Gilbert

Originated by Chroma Graphics Pte. Ltd
Printed and bound in China by
South China Printing Company

13 digit ISBN 978 1 406 20328 8 (hardback)
10 09 08 07 06
10 9 8 7 6 5 4 3 2 1

13 digit ISBN 978 1 406 20335 6 (paperback)
11 10 09 08 07
10 9 8 7 6 5 4 3 2 1

British Library Cataloguing in Publication Data
Thomas, Isabel, 1980–
    Shark vs. killer whale. – (Animals head to head)
    1. White shark – Juvenile literature
    2. Killer whale – Juvenile literature
    3. Animal fighting – Juvenile literature
    4. Predation (Biology) – Juvenile literature
    I. Title
    597.3'31566
A full catalogue record for this book is available from the British Library.

Acknowledgements
The publishers would like to thank the following for permission to reproduce photographs:

Alamy Images pp. **12** (George McCallum Photography), **13** (David Fleetham), **17** (Malcom Schuyl); Ardea.com pp. **14** (Kurt Amsler), **20** (Ron & Valerie Taylor), **24** (Francois Gohier); Corbis Royalty Free p. **16**; Corbis pp. **6** (Tom Brakefield), **21 right** (Stephen Frink), **25** (Mark A. Johnson), **28** (Jeffrey L. Rotman); DK Images p. **18**; FLPA pp. **4 right** (Malcom Schuyl), **8** (Minden Pictures/Norbert Wu); Getty Images/AFP p. **29**; Naturepl.com p. **19 right** (Jeff Rotman), **22** (Sue Flood), **26 right** (Brandon Cole); Photolibrary.com p. **4 left** (Ifa-Bilderteam Gmbh), **7** (Pacific Stock), **9** (Pacific Stock), **10** (Pacific Stock), **11** (Daniel Cox), **19 left** (Pacific Stock), **26 left** (Richard Packwood); Science Photo Library p. **21 left** (Eye of Science).

Cover photograph of a great white shark reproduced with permission of Photolibrary.com/Pacific Stock. Cover photograph of a killer whale reproduced with permission of FLPA/Minden Pictures/Flip Nicklin.

Disclaimer
All the Internet addresses (URLs) given in this book were valid at the time of going to press. However, due to the dynamic nature of the Internet, some addresses may have changed, or sites may have changed or ceased to exist since publication. While the author and publishers regret any inconvenience this may cause readers, no responsibility for any such changes can be accepted by either the author or the publishers.

Contents

Any words appearing in the text in bold, **like this**, are explained in the glossary.

Meet the contenders

A seal splashes into the sea. Hundreds of metres away a great white shark senses its **prey**. Seconds later the seal is caught in the shark's lethal jaws.

Further down the coast a group of seals plays on the beach. They are not as safe as they think. Without warning, an enormous killer whale lunges out of the waves. It grabs a seal from the sand, and then slides back into the icy ocean.

Killer whales might seem playful in zoos, but in the wild they are cruel and cunning hunters.

Sharks are feared as man-eaters, but they kill fewer than ten people a year.

Ocean killers

Killer whales (also called orcas) and great white sharks are two of the world's biggest ocean **predators**. They survive by hunting and eating other animals. Every part of a predator's body is designed to help it find, catch, and eat meat.

Great white sharks and killer whales are fearsome hunters. But which should be crowned the champion predator? To find out, let's compare their hunting and fighting skills.

This map shows where killer whales and great white sharks live in the wild.

KEY
- Killer whales
- Great white sharks
- Both killer whales and great white sharks

0   500   1000 Miles
0   500   1000 Kilometres

5

Size and agility

Sharks and killer whales both live in the sea and hunt the same **prey**, but they are very different. Sharks are **fish** that breathe underwater using **gills**.

Killer whales are **mammals** that live like fish. Their bodies are designed to help them move through the water. Killer whales look like fish but they have **lungs**, so they have to come to the surface to breathe air.

9.5 m (31 ft 2 in)

1.8 m
(5 ft 11 in)

Giant babies!
A newborn baby killer whale is as long as a car!

A male killer whale's fin is as tall as a man.

Massive meat-eaters

Sharks eat more meat than any other fish. They are so big they can eat almost anything, from small squid to huge sea mammals. Fishermen once caught a shark that had two whole sea lions in its stomach.

Killer whales are even bigger than great white sharks. A male killer whale can weigh the same as two elephants.

Enormous animals have the best choice of food. Killer whales are strong enough to knock seals off ice blocks in the sea. In groups, they can even attack a blue whale, which is the largest animal in the world!

Male great white sharks grow up to 6 metres (19 feet 8 inches) long.

1 m (3 ft 3 in)

6 m (19 ft 8 in)

Keeping warm

A shark's body temperature changes with the temperature of the seawater. Like other **mammals**, killer whales are able to keep their bodies warmer than the water they are in. This uses up a lot of energy, so orcas need to eat more often than sharks.

The oceans can get very cold, but a killer whale's large size helps it to stay warm. Big bodies lose heat slowly. A thick layer of fat called blubber protects the whales from injury and traps heat inside their bodies. It also stores energy for long journeys.

Useful blubber

Blubber helps killer whales to float and rest on the ocean surface. Sharks don't have blubber. They have to keep swimming or they will sink.

Some killer whales use their huge bodies to tip prey off ice blocks.

Strong but bendy

Great white sharks have the perfect combination of toughness and **agility**. Most **fish** have bony skeletons, but a shark has no bones. Its skeleton is made from **cartilage**. Cartilage is more bendy than bone, so a shark can twist and turn quickly.

A great white shark's nose is so tough it can damage boats!

HEAD TO HEAD

WINNER

	Killer whale	Shark	
Size	10	6	Shark is left feeling small.
Agility	7	9	Bones make whale less bendy.

9

Speed and stamina

A **predator's** body is designed to catch the kinds of **prey** found in its **habitat**. Killer whales and sharks are made for speed. They must attack quickly, or their prey will escape.

Sharks are **torpedo**-shaped swimming machines. Their powerful bodies are packed with muscles, but most of the time they move slowly to save energy. With a sudden flick of the tail they can reach top speeds of 40 km/h (25 mph).

Sharks attack so quickly that they burst out of the water.

Killer whales sweep their huge tails up and down to push themselves through the water. They cruise along at about 10 km/h (6 mph). When chasing prey they **accelerate** to almost 50 km/h (35 mph). The whale's smooth, **streamlined** body moves through the water easily.

Out of the blue

Killer whales often leap right out of the water. This is called breaching. Some killer whales are very clever and crash down on shoals of **fish**. This stuns the fish and makes them easy to catch.

Playful killer whales leap out of the water for fun.

Going the distance

Sharks and killer whales can travel huge distances when they hunt for food.

Great whites like to hunt near coasts, which is a problem for swimmers and surfers. But they also spend a lot of time far out at sea. Scientists tracked a great white shark that swam 7,000 km (4,350 miles) in one year!

Some killer whales live in large family groups and hunt in the same area all the time. Others **roam** hundreds of kilometres to find the best meals.

Big meal
Once a great white shark eats a seal or sea lion, it might not feed again for weeks.

Killer whales' tails are so powerful they can keep their bodies out of the water while they look around.

Deep sea diving

Because sharks have **gills**, they can hunt either at the surface or deep down in the cold, dark ocean depths. They can swim at depths of almost 2 kilometres (1.2 miles).

Killer whales have **lungs**. They like to breathe through their **blowholes** every 30 seconds, so they usually stay near the surface. But they can hold their breath for up to 15 minutes. This allows them to dive over 200 metres (650 feet) below the surface.

Gills only work if water is flowing over them. If a great white shark stops swimming it will die.

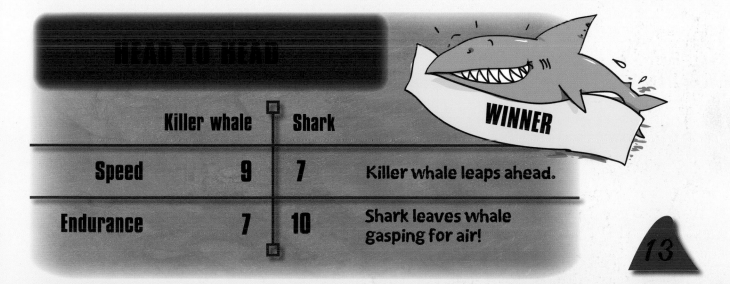

HEAD TO HEAD

	Killer whale	Shark	
Speed	9	7	Killer whale leaps ahead.
Endurance	7	10	Shark leaves whale gasping for air!

WINNER

13

A surprise attack

Sharp **senses** help a **predator** to find food and avoid enemies.

Shark attack

Great white sharks have incredible senses. They can hear injured fish that are several kilometres away. As they get closer, they start to smell their **prey**. A shark's brain can recognize different smells and work out where each one comes from.

Sharks have sensitive areas of skin that can detect tiny movements in the water. They can "feel" prey from 100 metres (330 feet) away, before they can see it. If an object looks like prey, a shark might bump into it to see if it could be food. If it seems tasty, the shark attacks.

A shark can see ten times better than us in the dark. This helps it to hunt at night or deep below the surface.

Deadly precision

As a great white lunges forwards, its eyes roll back into its head. Tiny **receptors** on the shark's nose guide the jaws to the right spot. These receptors detect signals from the victim's muscles. Even if the prey stays totally still, the shark can sense its heartbeat!

Taste is the final sense. If something tastes good the shark will come back for another bite!

Several kilometres away – sound

Several hundred metres away – scent

100 metres away – sensitive skin "feels" prey

Tens of metres away – sight

30 cm away – receptors on nose

0 cm away – taste and touch

All these senses work together to make sharks deadly predators.

15

Killer hearing

Killer whales have excellent hearing and use **echolocation** to track down **prey**. They make clicking sounds that travel through the water, bounce off nearby objects, and travel back towards the whale. By listening to these echoes, the whale can work out how big and how close its prey is.

Killer whales also have good eyesight. They often raise their bodies out of the water to see what is happening above the surface. This is called spy-hopping.

On the lookout
Great white sharks cannot spy-hop, but they do lift their heads out of the water to find large prey.

A killer whale's black and white patches fool prey into thinking it is a much smaller animal.

Shady tricks

Clever **camouflage** helps killer whales and sharks to stay out of sight as they approach prey. When seen from above, their dark-coloured backs blend into the gloom of the ocean. When seen from below, their white bellies make them almost invisible against the bright surface of the water. The unlucky prey does not see them coming until it is too late!

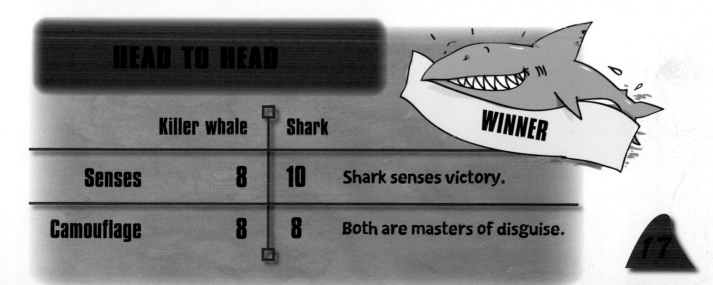

	Killer whale	Shark	
HEAD TO HEAD			**WINNER**
Senses	8	10	Shark senses victory.
Camouflage	8	8	Both are masters of disguise.

Deadly weapons

All **predators** use special weapons to catch and kill their food.

Tooth-packed jaws

Killer whales have up to 52 strong, cone-shaped teeth. When the whale clamps its mouth shut, the teeth fit closely together. They are perfect for grabbing slippery, speedy **prey** like **fish** and seals.

Great white sharks have a mouthful of deadly teeth. Each tooth is triangular and is sharp enough to slice through flesh and bone.

A killer whale's teeth grow up to 7 cm (2.5 inches) long.

A killer whale's teeth have to last a lifetime. But if a shark loses a tooth, a new one will grow. Great whites produce hundreds of new teeth every year. Each tooth grows up to 8 cm (3 inches) long.

Sharks and killer whales cannot chew food. They have to swallow their prey whole or tear off a mouthful.

Sharks sink their teeth into prey and shake their head quickly from side to side.

19

Bite force

Awesome jaws make a shark's bite deadly. Each tooth pierces a victim with enormous force. Great whites move their noses out of the way as they strike. Their jaws seem to pop out of their heads and reach towards the **prey**.

Killer whales also have huge jaw muscles to keep a tight grip on struggling prey. Their throats open wide enough to swallow a whole seal.

Bite and spit

Sometimes great white sharks bite a victim once and swim away to avoid a fight. Some prey animals are large, with dangerous teeth and claws. It is safer for the shark to return once the prey has bled to death.

This seal is recovering from a killer whale bite.

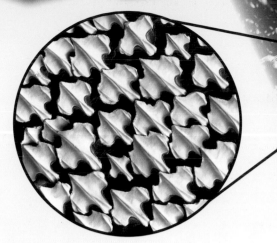

Toothy armour

Shark skin would feel smooth if you stroked it from head to tail. But stroking it back to front would make your hand bleed.

A great white's skin is covered in thousands of tiny scales, which are shaped like teeth. These point towards the tail, and help the shark to swim faster. They also protect it from injury.

A shark's skin is covered in super-hard scales.

HEAD TO HEAD

	Killer whale	Shark	
Teeth	8	10	Shark never needs a dentist!
Armour	6	8	Shark's prickly skin leaves whale blubbering...

WINNER

21

Hunting skills

We have seen what makes killer whales and sharks such fearsome **predators**.

Excellent **senses** help them track down food. **Stealth** and **camouflage** let them swim right up to victims without being seen. Powerful tooth-packed jaws make sure **prey** has no chance of escape.

Great white sharks and killer whales are similar in many ways, but their hunting methods are very different.

Killer whales call to each other to plan attacks.

Sneaky hunters

Sharks live and hunt on their own. They are masters of the surprise attack, rushing up from below or behind. They eat many different animals, from dolphins and porpoises to whale calves, **fish**, turtles, and squid.

Pod power

Killer whales live in family groups called **pods**. Each pod hunts together. When killer whales eat fish they use noisy calls and squeaks to plan their attacks. Pods that hunt **mammals** such as sea lions stay silent, so their prey doesn't hear them coming.

Top predators

Killer whales and sharks are at the top of their food chains. Few animals would dare to attack them!

A food chain shows who eats what in a habitat.

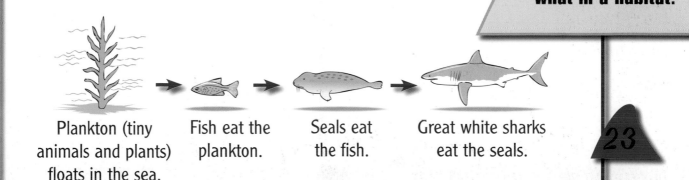

Plankton (tiny animals and plants) floats in the sea.

Fish eat the plankton.

Seals eat the fish.

Great white sharks eat the seals.

Killer cunning

Killer whales are clever hunters. Each **pod** learns the best way to catch the different foods in their **habitat**. Some groups herd fish close together to make them easy to catch. Others trap dolphins and penguins, or drown bigger kinds of whales by pushing them underwater.

When a killer whale learns a new trick to catch **prey**, it can teach the skill to the rest of its pod! Killer whales at Marineland in Canada have worked out how to trap seagulls. They spit **fish** out onto the water and wait under the surface for a bird to fly down – straight into their jaws.

Killer whales living near Argentina teach their babies to grab seals from the beach!

Man-eaters?

Sharks are born with fantastic hunting skills, but they do not learn as quickly as killer whales. Scientists think that great whites attack humans by mistake. From below, a surfer looks just like the shark's favourite prey.

Sharks prefer not to fight each other. They cannot hunt if they get hurt. When two sharks meet, the smaller one usually swims away. Big males might give rivals a quick nip to show off their strength.

Sharks don't like the taste of humans. But a person on a surfboard looks like a tasty seal or sea lion.

HEAD TO HEAD

	Killer whale	Shark	
Hunting skills	10	8	Killer whale finds strength in numbers.
Intelligence	10	6	You can't teach an old shark new tricks!

WINNER

25

Who wins?

Super **senses**, terrifying teeth, and strong bodies make killer whales and sharks fearsome **predators**. But which one wins?

Killer contest

Killer whales sometimes attack smaller sharks. A famous video shows a meeting between a killer whale and a great white shark near California, in the United States. The shark was attracted by the blood of a sea lion killed by the killer whale. As soon as the whale spotted the shark, it rammed into it at top speed. Tourists watched as the whale brought the shark to the surface in its jaws and began to thrash it around. In a few seconds, the shark was dead.

Scared away?

After this attack, all the sharks that lived in the area disappeared. Scientists think that the killer whales scared them away!

Bigger, faster, and smarter than a great white shark – the killer whale is the ultimate ocean predator.

HEAD TO HEAD

	Killer whale	Shark
Size	10	6
Agility	7	9
Speed	9	7
Endurance	7	10
Senses	8	10
Camouflage	8	8
Teeth	8	10
Armour	6	8
Hunting skills	10	8
Intelligence	10	6
Total	83/100	82/100

Killer whale splashes out on a victory party!

The real fight

Sharks and killer whales usually avoid each other. But they have a far more dangerous enemy to fear – humans.

Scientists believe that humans kill up to 100 million sharks every year. Many are killed by accident – they get caught in fishing lines or nets that protect swimmers. But many more are hunted on purpose. Great whites are killed for their fins, jaws, and teeth.

Hundreds of thousands of sharks are killed to make shark fin soup. Asian restaurants charge up to £56 ($100) per bowl. Laws are being introduced to protect sharks, but hunting is still a major problem.

Every year, hundreds of thousands of sharks are killed for their fins.

Habitats at risk

Ocean **habitats** are being destroyed. Humans catch the **fish** that sharks and whales eat. They also pollute the water with dangerous chemicals like **pesticides**. Small fish swallow these chemicals. When killer whales eat hundreds of these poisoned fish, they become sick and can die.

The **vibration** of noisy boat engines also makes it difficult for whales to **communicate** with each other.

It is difficult to count how many killer whales and sharks are left, but over 70 types of shark may soon become **extinct**. These awesome predators will only survive if they are treated with the respect they deserve.

Whales and sharks often die if they get caught in fishing nets.

29

Glossary

accelerate speed up

agility combination of speed and skill when moving

blowhole nostril in the top of the head of a whale or dolphin

camouflage body features that allow animals to blend into their habitat, to avoid being seen by predators or prey

cartilage tough but bendy tissue, found in the skeleton of sharks and in our nose and ears

communicate swap information

echolocation way in which whales find objects by giving out sounds and listening for the echoes that are reflected back

extinct when a type of animal no longer exists

fish animals with jaws, fins, scales, and gills, which live in water

gills body part that fish use to breathe

habitat place where an animal lives

lungs body part that mammals and other air-breathing animals use to breathe

mammal animal that can make its own body heat and produce milk for its babies

pesticide chemical used to kill pests such as insects

pod group of killer whales, often from the same family, that live together

predator animal that hunts, kills, and eats other animals

prey animal that is caught, killed, and eaten by another animal as food

receptors parts of an animal's body that are sensitive to changes in the surroundings

roam move over a large area

senses ways in which an animal gets information about its surroundings

stealth doing something slowly and quietly to avoid being noticed

streamlined smooth object that allows water to flow over it easily

torpedo missile that is launched from an aircraft, ship, or submarine and is designed to travel quickly underwater

vibration quick back and forth movement or shaking

More information

Books

Animals Under Threat: Great White Shark, Louise and Richard Spilsbury (Heinemann Library, 2004) focuses on the threats sharks face from humans.

Life in a pod: Whales, Louise and Richard Spilsbury (Heinemann Library, 2003) looks at how whales behave when they are living in a group.

Why am I a mammal?, Greg Pyers (Raintree, 2005) and *Why am I a fish?*, Richard and Louise Spilsbury (Raintree, 2005) will tell you more about the differences between sharks and whales.

Websites

www.nwf.org/wildlife/orca/ – this site will help you to become a killer whale expert with its amazing orca facts.

www.flmnh.ufl.edu/fish/Kids/kids.htm – visit this site for information about sharks and shark attacks, plus shark-based games to test your knowledge!

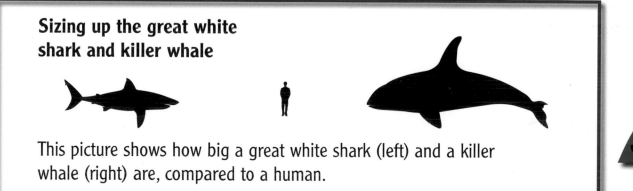

Sizing up the great white shark and killer whale

This picture shows how big a great white shark (left) and a killer whale (right) are, compared to a human.

Index